Y0-BDG-109

Stealth Invasion

Red Chinese Operations in North America

By Roger Canfield, Ph.D.

With an Introduction by Richard A. Delgaudio

United States Intelligence Council
Fairfax, Virginia

Cover photo by Richard A. Delgaudio©2001
Jacket design by John Conners

Books are available at special discounts for bulk purchases from the publisher. To order, please use the coupon on the last page of this book.

The United States Intelligence Council is incorporated under the IRS code as a 501(c) 4 corporation. USIC researches intelligence information important to the security, economic, national defense and independent sovereign interests of the United States, and disseminates this information to interested American citizens.

Printed in the United States of America

ISBN 0-9702053-1-7

8 7 6 5 4 3 2 / 03 02

Table of Contents

Introduction

I first met Dr. Roger Canfield as the author of a comprehensive study that I helped underwrite about radical New Leftists Jane Fonda and Tom Hayden, cheerleaders of America's enemies in Viet Nam. Since then Dr. Canfield and I have worked together on many conservative causes. Dr. Canfield is uncompromising on his principles and the truth. His research is always relentless and thorough. His writing clear and forceful. Dr. Canfield has a realist's view of the world. His intellect is sharpened by his military and political experience.

In the last two years, Dr. Canfield has meticulously researched and written three eye-opening monographs on the subject of Red China's war against America: the groundbreaking *What Red China Got for Its Money* (Why Did the People's Republic of China Invest in the 1996 Reelection Campaign of

President Bill Clinton?), *China Traders* (Assessing the Legacy of Clinton-Gore's Appeasement Policy: U.S. National Security at Risk), and this publication. In addition, he co-authored with me the widely distributed book, *China Doll: Clinton, Gore and the Selling of the U.S. Presidency* (more than 700,000 in print).

This report sketches the high points of his truly original research into the nearly 100-ship presence of the merchant marine of the People's Liberation Army — the China Ocean Shipping Company (COSCO). Dr. Canfield has found this agent of Beijing active in all major seaports serving North America, including Los Angeles, Long Beach, Oakland, Portland-Vancouver, Seattle, Tacoma, New Orleans, Houston, Miami, Charleston, Norfolk, Baltimore, New York-New Jersey, Halifax, Nova Scotia, and Panama City, Panama. His exhaustive research of open public sources and previously released classified materials integrate Chinese and U.S. web pages, business journals, government documents, and newspapers. Dr. Canfield has also visited several of these ports, in particular he was the co-host of the

2000 and 2001 missions to Panama with me, seeing firsthand how Red China has seized control of the strategic Atlantic and Pacific gateways to the Panama Canal.

After reading this report few will doubt that the presence of nearly 100 ships of Red China's merchant marine and millions of uninspected containers entering America is a clear and present danger to American lives and property on our home shores. Most will also conclude that routine security measures will be sufficient to greatly reduce such risks without harming civil liberties.

In the wake of the terrible assault on America of September 11, 2001 America's response has been twofold. First, we have gone after the enemy abroad in a battle which will go on for many years. Second, we have attempted to erect better defenses against those foreign enemies who want to kill Americans and hurt our economy, as they were so successful in doing on 9-11.

We hope America's policymakers will remember that Communist China has a far-too influential role in determining who and what enters America through our seaports, and that they will act to curtail that role and more closely monitor the China Ocean Shipping Company (COSCO), the "merchant marine of the People's Liberation Army of Red China." This book explains why that is vital for America's security .

Richard A. Delgaudio
Fairfax, Virginia
February 2002

Prologue

As thousands of U.S. Intelligence Council supporters who helped make this book possible know, I had researched and drafted *Stealth Invasion: Red Chinese Operations in North America* prior to the terrorist attacks on the World Trade Center and the Pentagon.

"Millions of Americans are today in harm's way on their own soil," I wrote before that fateful day, discussing what would prove to be a dark foreshadowing about the "high vulnerability of U.S. seaports to espionage and terrorism." I noted that "sloppy security" had already led to the "blood of sailors and the tears of families" in the case of the U.S.S. Cole in Yemen.

I now hope that the widespread distribution of *Stealth Invasion* and similar works by others will save American blood, treasure, and tears in years to come. Americans may have to confront

not only terrorists and their host states —
Afghanistan, Iraq, Iran, Syria, Libya, Sudan,
and North Korea — but also their arms suppli-
ers — the People's Liberation Army of the
People's Republic of China.

For the next stage might be biological, chemical, or nuclear weapons provided by Red
China to the state sponsors of terrorism.
Beijing's violations of nonproliferation treaties
continue to this day and remain a clear and
present danger.

Ominously, on the day al Qaeda terrorists
murdered thousands of innocent Americans,
Red China forged new relations with the
Taliban in Afghanistan.

May God keep you and yours vigilant and
free and give our leaders the wisdom to institute security measures that inconvenience us
without loss of our fundamental liberties.

Roger Canfield
Fair Oaks, California
February 2002

Chapter 1
Red China's 'Trojan Horse'

It is less noticed than Communist Chinese Generals sipping wine and eating tiny sandwiches in military exchanges at Harvard and the Pentagon. Though occurring in broad daylight and in morning fog every day of the year, it is a "stealth invasion" of America's shores at every major American seaport on the West, Gulf, and East Coasts.

The invasion force is a fleet of Red Chinese ships, the merchant marine of the People's Liberation Army (PLA), delivering millions of cargo containers of unknown content into the strategic waters of the U.S. every year. The sloppy security that killed 17 and injured 39 sailors on board the U.S.S Cole is worse in U.S. homeports. Millions of Americans are today in harm's way on their own soil.

Red Chinese vessels call unnoticed and un-inspected. Usually the China Ocean Shipping Company (COSCO) and its shadow, the Orient Overseas Container Line (OOCL) follow the rules and fill out the required paperwork. Instances of smuggling guns, drugs, technology, prostitutes, and labor are rare and seldom reported.

School children were once told the story of the wooden Trojan horse built by the Greeks to smuggle soldiers inside the walls of Troy. Today no one talks of the millions of sealed containers aboard Red Chinese ships, let alone their cross-continental distribution by railcar and truck trailer to every town in America. Only 2 percent of the containers are physically checked. An occasional story of drugs or human cargo makes the news. The high vulnerability of U.S. seaports to espionage and terrorism is seldom suspected and virtually never investigated.

Exposing the COSCO Threat

As opponent of the COSCO takeover of the Long Beach Naval Station, the U.S. Intelligence Council has long taken a particular interest in the security of U.S. seaports and home-based Naval forces. The successful terror attack upon the U.S.S. Cole has renewed USIC concerns — unfortunately in the price of the blood of sailors and the tears of families.

In 1997 Senator John McCain questioned the national security implications of a $157 million contract between COSCO and a Mobile, Alabama, shipbuilder. Yet several federal authorities told Congress that "COSCO represents no threat to our national security." Maritime Commission Chairman Harold J. Creel also denied any threat, but testified that COSCO engaged in bribes, kickbacks, and predatory pricing. "They are not profit-driven," he said. "They want to have their flag and their name on their ships."

Since the China Ocean Shipping Company is not driven by profits and is interested in flying the Red Chinese flag, it is clearly an agent of its master — The People's Liberation Army — and is an instrument of the military objectives of the People's Republic of China (PRC). Indeed, the PLA has forward deployed about 100 ships of its COSCO fleet into our waters.

One of COSCO's potential threats is its commingling with U.S. Navy ships within the waterways and chokepoints of strategic U.S. seaports. Since men and women of the U.S.S. Cole are dead and injured because of a mere rubber dinghy, it is prudent to watch the PLA deployment of COSCO's worldwide fleet of 600 vessels. It is rational and reasonable to improve security measures for vessels, facilities and citizens at American seaports where COSCO calls. Soon after the Cole disaster, the investigative TV show *Dateline* found it easy to move vessels among U.S. warships.

Other Threads of Beijing's Web

In addition to COSCO, the U.S. Intelligence Council recommends that U.S. intelligence and law enforcement agencies add the Beijing-dependent, Tung family-owned Orient Overseas Container Line (OOCL) to its watch list.

The U.S. Intelligence Council also wishes to alert authorities of the presence of Beijing-tied Li Ka-shing enterprises in the waterways of Vancouver-Seattle-Tacoma where the U.S. Navy homeports major submarine and destroyer forces and one aircraft carrier. USIC also recommends heightened security in those ports where Chinese commercial vessels — both COSCO and OOCL — commingle with the naval forces of the U.S. Navy, particularly in Seattle-Tacoma, Charleston, Norfolk, and Long Island Sound. USIC seeks measures to protect national security from COSCO and other PRC "front" companies such as Orient Overseas Container Line and Hutchison Whampoa.

Chapter 2
America's Achilles Heel: Poor Port Security

The little advertised, but long-named federal commission — the Interagency Commission on Crime and Security at U.S. Seaports — in the fall of 2000 completed an obscure report that ploddingly revealed shocking evidence of rampant crime, corruption, and sloth on security issues at major American seaports.

The Interagency Commission made on-site surveys of 12 seaports, of which seven — Charleston, Long Beach, Los Angeles, Miami,

New Orleans, New York/New Jersey and Tacoma — interest USIC because of COSCO's presence in those ports. In addition to these, this USIC report covers seaports in Portland, Seattle, Vancouver, New Orleans, Houston, Savannah, Norfolk, Halifax, and Baltimore, where the China Ocean Shipping Company and often the Orient Overseas Container Line offer shipping services.

After conducting its investigation, the commission reached the alarming conclusion that the state of security in these dozen major American seaports "ranges from poor to fair."

An independent FBI study reached a similar conclusion, ranking the vulnerability of our top 12 seaports to terrorist attack as "high." The Bureau's report adds that "such an attack has the potential to cause significant damage."

Indeed, only 2 percent of all trade cargo is physically inspected despite widespread evidence of inaccurate or misleading paperwork.

There is no excuse for this terrible lack of even the most rudimentary security precautions at the seaports and in waterways of the United States. This is a matter of great importance to our nation's security and economic interests. The failures of local and federal governments to have basic security safeguards in place are appalling.

Poor or even fair security is unwarranted given the importance of seaports to our national security and economic vitality:

- The U.S. Navy, Marine, Army or Air Force has facilities within five of the 12 ports surveyed by the Interagency Commission on Crime and Security at U.S. Seaports.

- Of the 13 seaports with additional obligations to be ready for a national military mobilization in a war or a crisis, the Interagency Commission studied four and found them all wanting in adequate security for a mobilization, lacking readiness exercises, and having incomplete vulnerability/threat assessments.

- Nine of 12 ports had "no waterside security measures" to protect from foreign vessels.

- Nine of 12 ports could be blocked at just one to three chokepoints.

- U.S. seaports have become critical chokepoints for future military mobilizations for overseas operations.

Rampant Crime on Our Waterfronts

While concerns for espionage or terrorism at seaports goes unaddressed, knowledge of crime waves on America's waterfronts has been known for perhaps a century. Massive underreported crime is known, but runs rampant on U.S. waterfronts.

Organized crime has little difficulty stealing cargoes and smuggling drugs or human beings. The Interagency Commission reported that organized crime is concealing drugs in cargoes at nine of the 12 ports it investigated. The Commission found that only three of 12 ports use modern technology to identify contraband or to verify shipments in suspicious cases only.

Criminally organized alien smuggling is common on the West Coast. Alien stowaways were found in 10 of 12 ports. "Immigration has no way of knowing whether manifested crews actually leave on the ship they arrive on ...or remain illegally in the United States." The CIA reported that about 50,000 women and children are lured to America annually and forced to work as abused laborers, servants and prostitutes, according to the *New York Times*. Some aliens had arrived from China in COSCO containers.

These vulnerabilities to crime are well known and their implications for organized espionage and terrorism ought to be transparent. The Royal Canadian Mounted Police, in their long-suppressed "Sidewinder" report, reveal intimate ties between Chinese Triad gangs and the Communist PRC. Clearly, American ports are open to theft of technology and destruction of human life and property and vital infrastructures.

In contrast to these street crimes, there is near total silence and little apparent action to explore vulnerability to espionage, export of militarily valuable technology or to terrorism.

Terrorism by the Shipload

Prior to the loss of 17 lives aboard a poorly secured U.S.S. Cole, the FBI told the Interagency Commission that the vulnerability of U.S. seaports to terrorist attacks was high, but said the terrorist threat was low. In other words, attacks upon U.S. ports were entirely in the hands of America's enemies who could choose the times and places of their attacks as long as our ports did nothing about their high vulnerability.

Eleven of 12 ports are located in urban areas where millions of innocent lives are in harm's way and where vital infrastructures (ports, roads, rail, telecommunications, water, electricity) are vulnerable to attack. Nuclear, biological, or chemical weapons — with or without missiles — might be secreted among the millions of cargo containers delivered to American ports on Red Chinese ships. Typically, ports lack basic intelligence information about terrorist threats provided to other agencies.

"Increasing awareness of security-related threats among port facilities ...and expanding the availability of threat information ...would do much to alleviate this problem....The federal government should establish baseline vulnerability and threat assessment for terrorism at U.S. Seaports."

The Interagency Commission said none of the dozen ports met "the minimum port security criteria." Only a third had barriers to halt or slow down a terrorist driving through fences. Half had "nonsecure" communications. With the exception of lighting and gates in most ports, persons and vehicles had easy physical access to most ports. Foreign sailors and domestic workers roam freely. Except for paper forms, foreign cargo is handled no differently than cargo from Kansas. It is inspected alongside domestic cargo in every port.

Smuggling Out U.S. Technology

"Seaports are vulnerable to those trying to acquire...weapons, munitions, and critical technology [that] affect national security." Federal inspectors working in remote locations spend more time behind computer terminals than on the docks. "The [Customs and

Commerce] inspection and criminal investigation personnel...devoted to export transactions are only a small fraction of those devoted to imports..." Shipper's Export Documents (SEDs), delivered as late as four days after a ship leaves port typically contain inaccurate, vague, misleading or false information.

No wonder that over two years (1996-98) in the 12 ports, the Commission reported only 296 offenses, 26 arrests, and 323 seizures valued at $33 million. "...[F]ederal agencies are probably detecting only a small portion of the controlled commodities that are being exported illegally," said the Commission. There is no criminal statute for illegal exports.

The unstated policy of local ports is perhaps "Don't ask," and the policy of intelligence agencies is "Don't tell." Our seaports are unaware of most security threats. The FBI, CIA, Customs, Coast Guard, local police and sheriff's office tells them little or nothing about possible security threats. Our seaports are not ready for prime time, not prepared for attacks like that on the U.S.S. Cole.

Nobody is looking. USIC urges the President, the Congress, and other government agencies to do their jobs defending national security. "Don't know and don't tell" is a dangerous policy of willful blindness. Our highly vulnerable seaports are open to Communist Chinese vessels every day in every port.

U.S. Customs Asleep on the Docks?

The U.S. Customs Service is responsible for border enforcement, having the authority to search any shipment that crosses the U.S. border. One duty of the Customs Service is to cooperate with the State Department's Office of Defense Trade Controls in conducting end-use checks of exports. The State Department sets criteria, but Customs carries them out.

Despite the congressional Cox report and other intelligence agency evidence, during the entire Clinton-Gore administration U.S. Customs Service indicted only one PRC entity for violating U.S. export laws. CATIC, the China Aero Technology Import and Export Corporation, was indicted for using U.S. B-1 and missile machine tools from McDonnell

Douglas to manufacture military aircraft and silkworm missiles in Nanchang. [*U.S. Customs Today*, January 2000].

Meanwhile, Customs devoted considerable resources to interdicting imports of drugs, child pornography, counterfeit clothing, bootleg software and forced labor goods.

Customs "discrepancy" statistics show China very faithfully following Customs' rules and regulations for processing paperwork. The China Ocean Shipping Company virtually never appears in U.S. daily newspapers, seldom in business journals, and infrequently in U.S. port websites. COSCO is virtually always below the radar screen. This stealth company quietly dominates container cargo ports throughout America. COSCO does not draw attention to itself and its routine commerce in the United States.

Though China (plus Hong Kong) was far and away the world's worst violator of slave labor, Customs reports in 1999 and 2000 "this merchandise...does not appear to be a large violation of the law." During those years, only 250 people had been prosecuted for slave trading, according to the 79-page report *"International Trafficking in Women to the United States: A Contemporary Manifestation of Slavery."* This is shocking, given the CIA's figure of 50,000 people who are brought here in secret bondage annually.

Customs vigorously moved to halt the import of Chinese artificial flowers, tea and other products through 20 detention orders and four findings in 1999. Meanwhile, Customs appeared to give scant resources and no mention on its website to preventing the export to China of U.S. nuclear, missile, stealth, fiber optic and other technologies vital to our nation's defense. Only one Chinese company and three foreign nationals were indicted.

U.S. Customs' automated export system flags all military goods destined for China and does not allow China a low value exemption from reporting detailed shipping information. Yet in fiscal 1999 Customs apparently found hardly any instances of violations that it con-

siders prosecutable except for the indictment
of three foreign nationals (fiber optic, stealth,
and antimissile technologies). [U.S. Customs,
FY 1999 Accountability Report].

Indeed, Customs has granted COSCO —
the nearly exclusive shipper to Communist
China and a Chinese government-owned
entity — special processing of its cargoes usually accorded to private and free world shippers. These privileges include automated
remote location filings and exemptions granted in early 1997 from submitting Cargo
Declarations with manifests and from present-
ing copies to Customs for review. Are such
efficiencies worth the national security risks of
potentially dangerous cargoes or exports of
militarily valuable technologies?

Another breach is opened by the freight
forwarder, the person often controlling the
shipping manifests or the paper trail on the
contents of ships and containers. Freight for-
warding is a legal business. The problem is the
loyalties of Red Chinese company owners.

Kenneth Timmerman writing in the October 1997 issue of the *American Spectator* lists as Red Chinese-controlled freight forwarders: Pan Ocean Lines, North China Cargo, CU Transport Inc. (a creature of the China National Foreign Trade Transportation Corporation) located in Alhambra, Rosemead, and Monterey Park, California. In Compton there's the China Interocean Transport Inc. (China National Foreign Trade Transportation Corp.); CCIC North America Inc. (China National Import and Export Commodities Inspection Corp.) in West Covina in El Monte, Morrison Express of El Segundo.

Timmerman's investigative reporting for *Readers Digest, American Spectator* and the Cox Report disclosed thousands of Red Chinese companies based in the U.S. — most in Los Angeles — that are open for business and possibly espionage. Under the 1999 Defense Authorization Act the Pentagon was ordered to identify Chinese front companies. It did not. Rep. Chris Cox, said, "The Clinton-Gore administration's failure to obey the law is knowing, willful and longstanding."

The whole Clinton-Gore response to Chinese espionage was bizarre, as described by Johnny Chung of *WorldNet Daily*: "This White House administration not only delivered Permanent Normal Trade Relations, but it also called Taiwan an intelligence threat to the U.S. and listed the country as a terrorist threat along with Russia, China, North Korea, Serbian-controlled Bosnia, Vietnam, Syria, Iraq, Iran, Libya and Sudan."

Meanwhile, the espionage threat of China inside the United States is unspoken and unexplored. We will concentrate most of our attention upon a Communist Chinese presence in U.S. seaports through Beijing's front companies.

Chapter 3
A Red Chinese Sailor in Every U.S. Port

The Red Chinese government owns the 600-ship China Ocean Shipping Company (COSCO), one of the world's largest container shipping enterprises. It operates as the merchant marine of the People's Liberation Army and as such has been caught transporting AK-47 automatic rifles to street gangs in Los Angeles, components of weapons of mass destruction to Iran, Iraq, Libya, North Korea. Yet COSCO has few critics and many friends.

The Many American Friends of COSCO

Old salts like my father, a career Navy man, remembered the days when signs saying "Dogs and Sailors Keep Off the Grass" littered the lawns of American harbor towns when swabbies "hit the beach." Those days are gone. There are far fewer American sailors now and Red Chinese sailors are welcomed everywhere. In Long Beach and Seattle locals ooze with affection for foreign sailors — in particular those from COSCO.

With help from the Clinton White House, the City of Long Beach tried mightily to give the former U.S. Naval Station to COSCO and local officials actively aided COSCO's quest for a larger (secure) facility in the region. For nearly three years, USIC and its over 350, 000 petition signers implored leaders to reconsider their short-sighted interest in trade. Finally, only acts of Congress nixed a 20-year lease of the Long Beach Naval Station to China and nudged the Port of Los Angeles out of a Pier 400 deal with COSCO. COSCO quietly stretched out at new berths at nearby Pier J.

In the Los Angeles region proponents of increasing trade with China have largely silenced debate about the strategic importance of the Ports of Long Beach and Los Angeles to the nation's security.

COSCO's Beijing website happily exclaims: "On May 8, [2000] the Long Beach Port Authority held a ceremony in HYATT Hotel for President Chen Zhongbiao of COSCO Group, in which President Chen got the honorary Long Beach Pilot Award. During the ceremony, Madam O'neill [sic], the mayor of Long Beach, expressed her sincere thanks for President Chen's support for the establishment of friendly cooperation between COSCO and Long Beach, especially under the complicated situation two years ago. The Chairman of Long Beach Port Committee song [sic] high praise for President Chen's superior working style and his devotion to the development of shipping industry of China and the U.S., and even the whole world. After the speech, he awarded President Chen the honorary Long Beach Pilot Award on behalf of Long Beach Port Authority."

Still the City and Port of Seattle far surpasses the Long Beach kowtow. Seattle perfected genuflection with uniforms and music provided by — one presumes — a reluctant U.S. Navy. Locals persuaded a U.S. Navy band to provide uniforms and music. One suspects the Navy was keelhauled, dragooned, and impressed against its will.

Commemorating the glorious 20th anniversary of the China trade with Seattle in April 1999, a "...fireboat fired towering columns of water...a 13th [U.S.] Naval District band broke into 'It's a Small World.' The red and gold flag of the People's Republic of China and the Stars and Stripes were raised and snapped together..."

"There is a larger meaning...connections with...one of the leading countries of the world in the next century," said Port of Seattle Commission President Patricia Davis. "[The] ...arrival of each COSCO ship...[is]...vital for world stability and security and prosperity...." [*Seattle Post-Intelligencer*, April 19, 1999].

So what is COSCO? What's the problem with thousands of jobs and billions of dollars of trade with China?

A Vast Shipping Empire

COSCO is "one of the world's largest shipping lines, with more than 600 vessels, several hundred [300] subsidiary companies and [has] 80,000 employees handling trade in 150 countries," said Seattle-based COSCO spokesman Mike Foley in the April 19, 1999 issue of the *Seattle Post-Intelligencer.*

According to its website "COSCO Group ships visit more than 1200 ports." Of COSCO's vast fleet, close to 100 ships call on U.S. ports, and about 300 use the Panama Canal. Its larger container vessels have a capacity of 5250 TEUs (20-foot equivalent container units). In 1997, the volume of cargo carried by COSCO's world container fleet was 3.4 million TEUs over 653.4 billion ton-miles.

Headquartered in Beijing, COSCO Group has major offices in Hong Kong, Japan,

Singapore, the United States, Europe, South Africa and Australia. China Ocean Shipping Company Americas, Inc., has over 85 subsidiaries and offices throughout the American continent with over 700 employees. COSCO Americas Inc. is headquartered in Secaucus, New Jersey.

This shipping enterprise is listed as a "red chip," a PRC-owned company, on the Hong Kong Stock exchange [*Reuters*, May 15, 2000] and is seeking a co-listing on New York exchanges. COSCO floats loans in American markets. Recently, COSCO Group Ltd appointed BankBoston NA to arrange a $50 million loan to refinance debt. [*Bloomberg News* May 9, 2000].

COSCO has an increasingly routine presence in America's ports. Its ships sail in and out of American ports every day — Baltimore, Charleston, Houston, New York, Miami, New Orleans, Norfolk, Oakland, Port Elizabeth (NJ), Portland (OR), Seattle and Tacoma.

Even Washington, D.C., has noted COSCO's presence — although not in the form of a fleet on the Potomac. Under the adept leadership of Rep. Christopher Cox (R-Ca.), Congress issued a highly revealing report of Communist Chinese theft of U.S. nuclear secrets and access to U.S. missile guidance technology, which just happened to mention a certain shipping operation.

"The China Ocean Shipping Company (COSCO), the PRC's state-owned shipping company... operates under the direction of the Ministry of Foreign Trade and Economic Cooperation and answers to the PRC State Council," the congressional report stated.

The Clinton-Gore administration suppressed further information within the full-classified Cox report: "The Clinton administration has determined that additional information concerning COSCO that appears in the Select Committee's classified Final Report cannot be made public..."

Perhaps the Bush administration will see fit to reveal more about COSCO than did his kow-towing predecessor. "Although presented as a commercial entity," according to the House Task Force on Terrorism and Unconventional Warfare, "COSCO is actually an arm of the Chinese military establishment."

Chapter 4
The PLA's Merchant Marine

The China Ocean Shipping Company's civilian trappings and predominately commercial enterprises obscure its military mission.

The China Ocean Shipping Company, COSCO, is the merchant marine of the People's Liberation Army (PLA) of the People's Republic of China (PRC). The PRC refers to COSCO ships as *zhanjian* or "warships" and boasts that COSCO workers are and will be ready for battle into the next century.

The Communist Chinese government owns it. COSCO Beijing's website carries quotations from top Communist Party officials. COSCO is intimately linked to the China International Trust and Investment Corp. (CITIC), a key fundraiser for the Chinese government and a technology-acquiring source for China's military. COSCO serves its master.

An article in the November 10, 1997, *New American* described COSCO as "hardly a typical state-owned shipping company. COSCO ships have been used to ferry tanks to the Marxist regime in Burma, ship North Korean rocket fuel to Pakistan, smuggle heroin into Canada, ship AK-47s bound for California street gangs, technology smuggling to China." It has even purchased a Russian K-3 nuclear attack submarine from Finland.

Espionage and Other Clandestine Activities

Indeed, COSCO ships have been caught and cited for transporting components of weapons of mass destruction such as Chinese missile technology, and nuclear, chemical, and biological weapons components, materials and fuels into North Korea, Pakistan, Syria, Iraq and Iran, according to U.S. intelligence and international authorities. COSCO has been repeatedly cited over many years and as recently as late 1999.

More ominously for our national security, COSCO is "known to be associated with Chinese intelligence operations," according to the bestseller by Edward Timperlake and William Triplett, *Year of the Rat.* Like Soviet trawlers before them, COSCO ships sail in the waterways and dock at strategic locations all across the globe and in every major American port. These locations enable them to intercept electronic communications everywhere.

Li Ka-shing, COSCO senior advisor and owner of Hutchison Whampoa (operators of ports worldwide) "is to the Chinese army intelligence HQ what Howard Hughes was for the CIA," says William Triplett, author of *Red Dragon Rising.*

Recently, the Chinese were caught monitoring Japanese radio signals and mapping

undersea approaches to Japan for their sub-
marines. In July 2000 a secret CIA report
described Russian merchant ships gathering
signals intelligence north of Puget Sound and
the Ports of Seattle and Tacoma. It is prudent to
presume that — like the Soviets and the
Russians — the Chinese are gathering intelligence in America with their forward deployed
assets — COSCO ships and agents.

Smuggling is another activity in which
COSCO vessels have been employed, transporting contraband weapons, drugs, slave
labor, and prostitutes.

Richard Delgaudio testified before a U.S.
Senate Armed Services Committee hearing
chaired by Sen. John Warner, that Li Ka-shing
is "China's Red Billionaire" and his firm is
deeply involved in clandestine operations for
Red China's military. Delgaudio's testimony
and his book *Peril in Panama* amply document
China's threats to the Panama Canal and to the
U.S. from missiles smuggled into Li's port facilities there.

The *New American* calls COSCO "a PLA-connected container shipping fleet that specializes in drug and weapon smuggling." COSCO smuggled 2,000 AK-47 assault rifles into San Francisco in 1996 — the largest seizure of smuggled automatic weapons in U.S. history. Smuggled aboard the COSCO vessel *Empress Phoenix,* the weapons were "destined for Asian street gangs founded by illegal immigrants who were once members of the PLA's elite Red Guard," according to the *New American.*

Added Canada's *Globe and Mail* in a May 4, 1996 story: "Top officials of the two Beijing-based companies Norinco and Poly Technologies that make weapons for the Chinese military participated in the smuggling."

In February 1996, President Clinton met with Poly Technologies Chairman Wang Jun after taking a donation from Charlie Trie. A Rand report says, "Wang Jung is both director of CITIC and Chairman of Poly Group, the arms trading company of the General Staff Department."

Wang Jun's employer of record is COSCO, according to the *New American.* Wang Jun, the chairman of the Poly Group is a business partner with Ng Lap Seng, described by the *New American* as a "Macau mobster," who in turn is a business partner with Macau casino king Stanley Ho and, through Charlie Trie, a conduit of other Chinese money to Clinton and Gore.

"Poly's U.S. subsidiaries were abruptly closed in August 1996," states a Rand report. "Allegedly, Poly's representative, Robert Ma, conspired with China North Industries Corporation's (NORINCO) representative, Richard Chen, and a number of businessmen in California to illegally import 2000 AK-47s into the United States." Their customers were undercover U.S. Customs and BATF agents.

A year later, after Senator John McCain questioned an above-market and taxpayer-subsidized COSCO contract for $157 million with a Mobile Alabama shipbuilder, the CIA, the Coast Guard, and the Customs Service told congressmen Steve Horn and David Dreier that, "COSCO represents no threat to our national security." [*Washington Times*, April 4, 1997].

Harold J. Creel, Maritime Commission chairman, did admit that COSCO engaged in bribes, kickbacks, and predatory pricing. "They are not profit-driven. ...They want to have their flag and their name on their ships," said Creel.

Today the China Ocean Shipping Company has become a dominant force in modern container shipping in the world while the U.S. retreats from maritime activities vital to its own defense.

Chapter 5
Surrendering the High Seas

In contrast to the China Ocean Shipping Company's massive merchant marine fleet, the U.S. Navy Military Sealift Command operates only 110 ships across the globe. While these ships are identified as "U.S.NS" — United States Naval Ships — they are not commissioned ships of the U.S. Navy. Civilians man U.S. sealift ships, not military personnel. However, COSCO's large fleet is under the absolute control of the People's Liberation Army.

Most U.S. sealift vessels are in reserve and require time to activate. The National Defense Reserve Fleet (NDRF) has activated up to 600 ships to meet sealift needs during the Korean War, Berlin Crisis, Suez Crisis, Vietnam War, and to ship coal to Europe and grain to India.

These historically proven needs aside, "Currently, the NDRF consists of [only] 258 vessels…. However, 85 are no longer militarily useful and are slated for scrapping. In addition …another 51 ships are held…on a reimbursable basis. Forty-one of these are naval vessels awaiting disposal. These vessels are maintained at Benicia (Suisun Bay), California; Beaumont (Neches River), Texas; and Fort Eustis (James River), Virginia and at designated outported berths." [U.S. Department of Transportation, Bureau of Transportation Statistics, Maritime Administration, U.S. Coast Guard *Maritime Trade and Transportation 1999*, BTS99-02, Washington, DC: 1999].

Thus America's available defense reserve fleet now comprises 143 ships — far less than the 600 found necessary several times since

World War II and about equal to the COSCO fleet servicing just U.S. seaports.

In addition, American capacity to draw upon private U.S. shippers is quite limited. "U.S.-flag oceangoing vessels play a small role in carrying the nation's international commerce. ...the United States ranks 26th in the number of [U.S. flagged] ships and 11th in total DWT...The United States ranks 13th in the number of tankers, 9th in tanker DWT, 8th in containerships, and 6th in containership DWT." While approximately 45 percent of the world fleet by deadweight capacity calls at U.S. ports, most is carried in foreign — increasingly Red Chinese — ship bottoms. (*U.S. Industry and Trade Outlook* 1998)

China Leads the Container Revolution

Enclosed 20- and 40-foot-long metal containers are increasingly the standard of efficiency. Most containers are truck trailer sized bodies easily moved from truck to railcar to ship. Containers ease storage, retrieval, and transfers of bulk cargo among ship, railcar or truck, but they are major security problems.

Drugs, weapons, and human beings are easily hidden from view and closed containers are difficult to inspect.

The latest containerships have a capacity of 4,500 20-foot equivalent container units (TEUs) or more, and require drafts of 40 to 46 feet when fully loaded.

"To physically accommodate megaships at U.S. ports, channel and berth depths must be at least 50 feet. However, only five of the top 15 U.S. container ports — Baltimore, Tacoma, Hampton Roads, Long Beach, and Seattle — have adequate channel depths, and only those on the west coast have adequate berth depths. In addition, ports may need to expand terminal infrastructure, such as cranes, storage yards, and information systems, to facilitate the increased volumes of cargo from these ships. Also, landside modes and facilities ...will face higher volumes of rail and truck traffic. Many ports have initiated expansion projects to accommodate these ships." (U.S.DOT MARAD 1998, 49-51).

Local port expansion projects of over a billion dollars are common as U.S. ports compete to accommodate new container traffic — much of it by Beijing-owned COSCO and the Beijing-friendly Orient Overseas Container Line, (OOCL). While using taxpayer funds is common, the use or swapping of former military port facilities is well hidden. (Long Beach, Oakland, Charleston, New York, Newport).

The world's containership fleet increased 15 percent annually from 1993 to 1997 as the larger ships handling 4,000 or more 20-foot equivalent container units came into service mostly in east/west trade.

Who is building the ships? Japan and South Korea alone build a third. China may be a distant third, but the U.S. ranks 14th, accounting for an anemic 1 percent of gross tonnage of ships built.

In late September 2000 the *Washington Times* discovered a Clinton Pentagon proposal to build American auxiliary military ships overseas. After protests from Congress, Rear Adm.

Craig Quigley claimed that Clinton's Defense Secretary William Cohen had "emphatically not" supported the idea. The only remaining support ship builders in the U.S. are National Steel in San Diego and Avondale Industries in New Orleans. American shipbuilders shrunk from 21 firms in the 1980s to six defense ship-yards in 2000.

Foreign flagged, built, and manned vessels are landing on U.S. coasts — 42 percent of the value of U.S. waterborne trade hit the West Coast, 38 percent the East, and 18 percent the Gulf in 1997. (U.S.DOC Census 1997, table 1069; U.S.DOT MARAD 1998). COSCO leads this foreign armada.

Long Beach and Los Angeles dominate West Coast trade, but waterways contiguous to the ports of Vancouver, B.C., Seattle and Tacoma are strategic assets for U.S. Navy operations on the Pacific Rim. The port of New York/New Jersey leads the East Coast in both value ($68 billion) and in containers (1.7 million TEUs) handled in 1997, but Charleston and Norfolk are major container ports. The Gulf ports of

Houston and South Louisiana handle bulk commodities and crude petroleum making them the top two U.S. ports by gross tonnage.

COSCO's Role in Red China's Naval Warfare Strategy

Evidence suggests COSCO plays a greater role as a "naval arm" of the People's Liberation Army of the People's Republic of China far beyond that of merchant marine.

"There is a consensus among military specialists that China is prioritizing two areas of military growth: its missile program and its navy," states the authors of *Year of the Rat.* "COSCO is essential to its naval program."

Red China seems to be preparing to contest with the U.S. Navy, Taiwan, and Japan in its own region. Six hundred COSCO merchant vessels do not appear as major combatants in that theater. However, they perform other functions of naval strategy — COSCO is China's forward-deployed naval forces across the globe.

Chinese naval strategy for COSCO might be described as follows:

Some vessels could serve as platforms for theater ballistic missiles as well as containers for nuclear, biological and chemical weapons. They might provide mobile bases for the cyber-war much discussed as part of China's RMA (Revolution in Military Affairs).

Ships equipped with electronic information gathering devices can provide signals intelligence from every important U.S. seaport.

Richard Delgaudio in *Peril in Panama* shows how COSCO can secretly deploy an intermediate range nuclear missile at Li Ka-shing's Panama ports to threaten 100 or more major U.S. cities.

And COSCO might conceivably serve as an expeditionary force projecting military power far from China.

The U.S. Navy describes naval forces as "sea-based, self-contained, and self-sustaining...relatively unconstrained by regional infrastructure requirements or restrictions. Further, naval forces can exploit the freedom of maneuver afforded by the seas...

"*Mobility and Adaptability.* Naval forces can operate anywhere on the oceans, free of diplomatic restraint. As such, they have an unmatched ability to operate forward continuously, react to contingencies... and act as the enabling force for follow-on Army and Air Force power...

"*Presence and Visibility.* Ships can be purposely conspicuous or exceptionally difficult to detect. In peacetime, ...visibility...signal[s] interest, readiness, and ability to act if a crisis brews. The same ships, stationed close in, on the horizon, just over it, or in unlocatable places and circumstances, can be used as needed in crisis or conflict. With the ability to cumulate forces, naval power can be adjusted or scaled at will, increasing or decreasing pressure...as...leadership chooses to raise or lower...commitment, and engage or disengage much more easily than land-based forces, ...

"The enduring attractiveness of naval power is the flexibility that stems from these inherent characteristics and attributes. Investments in the Navy and Marine Corps are like money in the bank. We do not need to know precisely how and where we will use this resource in order to see its value — indeed our value is greater because we are useful virtually anywhere and anytime. Our expeditionary character, mobility, adaptability, variable visibility, and cooperative and independent capabilities....an especially relevant and useful force. Entering this new century, the technology, information, strike and telecommunications revolutions are rapidly undoing ...bounds on naval power. ...Communications capacities...have increased by several orders of magnitude. Information processing capabilities have expanded concomitantly. Sensor and surveillance systems provide ship-based forces with information about and insights into the land environment that can equal that of land-based forces. [U.S. Navy, Posture Statement 2000]."

The China Ocean Shipping Company's vast fleet already enjoys both the classic advantages and the modern application of all naval vessels outlined above. And it also benefits from the support of some very influential allies around the world.

Chapter 6
COSCO's Network of Powerful Allies

The China Ocean Shipping Company does not have to conduct its mission alone. In addition to its expanding web of operations in North America and around the world, COSCO can rely on a network of influential "friends." The surprising range of connections include a Chinese billionaire whose Hong Kong-based company operates ports around the globe, a former U.S. Secretary of State, and a "shadow" container company bailed out by a member of the Chinese mafia.

The 'Red Billionaire'

In *Perils in Panama* and in testimony before the U.S. Senate, USIC Chairman Richard Delgaudio has detailed the career and activities of Li Ka-shing. A plastic flower manufacturing king, Li met Y. K. Pao, a Hong Kong banker, who introduced him to banker Michael Sandberg. Sandberg was looking for a Chinese businessman with the best *guanxi* to the Beijing leadership. Li was just the right man. Sandberg helped Li get a bargain price for his bank's 22 per cent stake in a British owned *hong* — Hutchison Whampoa.

By late 1999, a secret "Intelligence Assessment" by the U.S. Southern Command Joint Intelligence Center, said, "Li Ka-shing, Hutchison Whampoa's owner, has extensive business ties in Beijing and has compelling financial reasons to maintain a good relationship with Beijing. ...Hutchison's containerized shipping facilities in the Panama Canal, as well as the Bahamas, could provide a conduit for illegal shipments of technology or prohibited items from the west to the PRC, or facilitate the movement of arms and other prohibited items into the Americas."

Li Ka-shing's vast global shipping empire requires watching because of his intimate connection to COSCO as its Honorary Senior Advisor. COSCO Beijing website says:

"Mr. Li is one of Hong Kong's most prominent businessmen; as Chairman & Managing Director of Cheung Kong Holdings and Hutchison Whampoa Ltd., Hong Kong he requires no forther [sic] introduction."

China military specialist William Triplett, co-author of *Red Dragon Rising,* describes Li as "the banker" for the Chinese army. The Rand Corporation, the U.S. Bureau of Export Affairs, and the U.S. Embassy in Beijing, all report that Li Ka-shing and his companies serve the Chinese military as financiers and acquirers of high technology for the PLA. [Charles Smith, *WorldNet Daily*]

Li Ka-shing is also a major investor in the China International Trust and Investment Corporation (CITIC). Both the White House in

1994 and the Rand Corporation in 1997 revealed Li Ka-shing's role in CITIC. According to the 1994 White House dossier, Li Ka-shing is a member of the boards of directors of the China International Trust and Investment Corporation. The CITIC bank is also more than it seems. The Rand report said, "CITIC does enter into business partnerships with and provide logistical assistance to PLA and defense-industrial companies like Poly (Technologies)." Poly Technologies, Ltd. is the primary commercial arm of the PLA General Staff Department's Equipment Sub-Department. CITIC, according to the Rand Corporation, "became identified with the PLA as a result of the scandal surrounding (Poly Technologies chairman) Wang Jun and his visit to the White House on 6 February 1996." [Charles Smith, *WorldNet Daily*]

According to a 1994 Clinton dossier provided to participants in a trade mission, Li has "significant economic and political ties to China," including investments in a "power station, a highway construction project and a large contribution to Shantou University." [Charles Smith, *WorldNet Daily*].

In 1997, the Rand Corporation's secret report on the "Chinese defense industry" revealed, according to Charles Smith, Li Ka-shing's direct connections to the Chinese military. "Hutchison Whampoa of Hong Kong, controlled by Hong Kong billionaire Li Ka-shing, is also negotiating for PLA wireless system contracts, which would build upon his equity interest in (Chinese army) Poly-owned Yangpu Land Development Company."

A U.S. Intelligence Council search of recent financial and stock market news reveals Li Ka-shing, his family, and his companies heavily invested in the Internet, telecommunications, electricity, and water. China's new military doctrines — a Revolution in Military Affairs (RMA) — advocate cyberwar against the internet and disruptions of telecommunications. This doctrine taken with the Chinese appreciation of the vulnerability of infrastructures is disturbing — given its possible use of agents to exploit Li Ka-shing in strategic industries and locations around the world. Prudent intelligence services ought to watch.

COSCO senior advisory board member, Li Ka-shing, has his own shipping empire mostly concentrated in port facilities used by COSCO outside of the United States. Li's principal property holding company Cheung Kong owns a maritime arm through Hutchison Port Holdings Ltd. (HPH). HPH has 18 major ports around the world (4 in the UK alone) and 8 other affiliates. Li's companies recently handled 10 percent of the world's global shipments.

Hong Kong International Holdings (HIT) operates at Container Terminals 4, 6, 7 and through its joint venture with China Ocean Shipping Company (COSCO) at Terminal 8 East. In 1996, HIT was offered the right to develop and operate two berths in Container Terminal 9 (CT9). HPH owns three other incomplete container terminals in Hong Kong, is purchasing port facilities at the Suez Canal, owns Frazer docks in Vancouver, and has interests in other shipping container companies. Li Ka-shing's container facilities include: Freeport Container Port, Bahamas; Panama Ports Company, Balboa & Christobal; UK -Port of Felixstowe; Harwich International Port; Thamesport; Europe Combined Terminals, Rotterdam; Port Said, Eygpt; Jakarta International Container Terminals; Jakarta's Koja Container Terminal; Myanmar International Terminals (Burma); Thilawa, Yangon.

In mainland China Li Ka-shing operates: Shanghai Container Terminals; Yantian International Container Terminals, Shenzhen; Nanhai International Container Terminals; Jiangmen International Container Terminals; Zhuhai International Container Terminals (Jiuzhou); Shantou International Container Terminals; Xiamen International Container Terminals; Zhuhai International Container Terminals (Gaolan); Hong Kong International Terminals; NigboPort.

A Former Secretary of State

Li serves with General Alexander M. Haig, Jr. as a COSCO advisor, according to the COSCO Beijing website in the first week of June 2000. The former NATO Commander, Secretary of State, Presidential Chief of Staff, has been a paid "domestic and overseas senior honorary advisor" to the China Overseas Shipping Company. He lobbied to obtain the Naval Station in Long Beach for the Chinese.

As owner of Worldwide Associates, Haig advises United Technologies, a manufacturer of jet engines, air conditioners, and elevators. The company has made billions of dollars in 17 joint ventures in China. It is reminiscent of Armand Hammer's exclusive franchises in the Soviet Union for pencils, asbestos, chemicals, artwork, banking, medicines, and oil.

Haig's backing of China trade extends to newspaper columns and expert commentary on television. *McAlvany Intelligence* reports, "Haig has been...aggressive in defending the Red Chinese butchers... defending the Red Chinese leaders just a few months after they slaughtered up to 10,000 student demonstrators in 1989. When China (in early '96) blockaded the Taiwan Straits and lobbed nuclear capable missiles . . . off the coast of Taiwan . . . and threatened to nuke Los Angeles if America came to the aid of Taiwan, Haig frantically called members of Congress, defending China and urging [Congress] not to impose trade sanctions...."

Haig is just one of six former Secretaries of State who publicly support permanent normal trading relations with China.

The "Shadow" Company

According to the Royal Canadian Mounted Police, Li Ka-shing is very connected to Tung Chee-hwa, the Beijing appointed Chief Executive of Hong Kong and shares many ventures with the Tung family company Orient Overseas Container Line (OOCL).

"Orient Overseas owns a 23 percent stake in $1.8 billion Oriental Plaza, in Beijing ...backed by the Tungs, Richard Li (Pacific Century) and Li Ka-shing (Hutchison)," [*Business Week* March 24, 1997; *22nd March 1999.* ...June 1999 Issue Paul Money].

The brothers Tung of Hong Kong have a successful family business and profitable political relations with Beijing. Younger brother C.C.

Tung, chairman of the OOCL since 1996, is a member of advisory boards for both COSCO and the Panama Canal. Rescued from bankruptcy by Beijing and Li Ka-shing, C.C.'s older brother Tung Chee-hwa was CEO of Orient Overseas until he was chosen by Beijing to run Hong Kong as its chief executive after the Communist takeover in July 1997. Despite Tung's high position, a man named Henry Fok may really be "the puppet master in Hong Kong."

In 1986 when Tung Chee-hwa's OOCL shipping business was on the brink of bankruptcy owing some $2.7 billion to its creditors, Red Chinese interests came up with the $120 million he needed to stay in business. They restructured $1.6 billion in debt and declared $1 billion of it as equity. Henry Fok, identified by the U.S. Justice Department as a member of the Chinese Triad and a Hong Kong businessman with extensive ties to the Red Chinese mainland, engineered the deals to bail out OOCL.

It is widely believed that Henry Fok brokered bridge loans from Li Ka-shing and PLA-owned COSCO to keep Orient Overseas afloat. Fok was a decades-long Communist Party activist who assisted the PRC during the Korean War. [Chapter 8, *The Year of the Rat*]. "Further support for Tung in Peking came from Li Ka-shing, who also helped rescue Orient Overseas." [Dr.Karl-Heinz Ludwig Ursulastr. 5 D - 80802 MÜNCHEN].

According to the *Far Eastern Economic Review*, Fok and his Red partners invested still again two years after the bailout, "giving them a key role in the restructuring of the Tung empire." Though having a financial stake in Orient Overseas International, they allowed Tung to recover equity very quickly. In 1987 Tung's wealth was "peanuts." A vehicle called Tung Holdings Trust, THT, held 65 percent of the company that controlled 74.6 percent of Orient. Fok acquired 27.48percent of THT in 1989. In 1991 Tung borrowed to buy back 23 percent from Fok. In 1992 debts were converted to Tung shares of Orient Overseas. By 1996 Tung had recovered 57.6 percent of a now very profitable company.

One well-placed source (he asks to remain nameless when discussing Fok) says: "Henry Fok could become the next leader of Hong Kong just by asking the Chinese for it." But Fok seems to have concluded that he can exercise all the power he wants through his man, Tung Chee-hwa, while maintaining the very low profile he craves." [Nov 18, 1996 *Forbes Today*].

His financial future secure and his loyalty certain, Beijing appointed Tung Chee-hwa to become Hong Kong's executive officer and his brother C.C. Tung took over OOCL in October 1996. ["Henry Who: A Friend Indeed," By Simon Fluendy, *Far Eastern Economic Review,* January 9, 1997; *Fortune* April 1, 1996].

In late June 2000 the *South China Morning Post* reported that Chinese leaders in Beijing "told a group of visiting Hong Kong tycoons they should support Hong Kong Chief Executive Tung Chee-hwa for a second term in exchange for favorable business treatment." The paper's largest shareholder, Robert Kuok, complained that the reporter, Willy Lam, didn't appreciate "manifestations of patriotism to the mother." [*Reuters*, Nov 4, 2000]. Chinese President Jiang Zemin "lashed out at journalists for asking whether Tung was the 'emperor's choice' to serve for another five-year term," reported *Reuters* on Nov 11, 2000. Demoted as China editor, Lam resigned.

A Beijing-revitalized Orient Overseas Container Line is back as "one of the world's largest international integrated containerized businesses," according to its website. In 2000 OOCL had 13 offices and very extensive business activities in the People's Republic of China and 160 offices in 50 countries.

With 21 branches in China, OOCL "covers virtually every province and major trade center." OOCL calls at 13 Chinese ports — Dalian, Fuqing, Fuzhou, Huangpu, Ningbo, Qingdao, Shanghai, Shantou, Shekou, Taiping, Xiamen, Xingang and Yantian. Li Ka-shing operates many of these ports including Shanghai Yantian, Shantou, Xiamen, and Nigbo.

In the United States OOCL operates in many of the same ports as COSCO. OOCL in

America is headquartered in the San Francisco-Oakland Bay area town of Pleasanton. OOCL has service offices in the coastal cities of Boston, Charleston, Houston, Long Beach, New York, Seattle and in Vancouver, B.C. and Panama. In addition to services in cities with OOCL offices, OOCL ships also deliver cargoes to Savannah, Norfolk, Miami, Los Angeles, and Oakland.

OOCL owns Long Beach Container Terminal, berths 6-10 at Pier F in Long Beach, Global Terminal in New Jersey, Howland Hook on Staten Island New York, and Deltaport and Vanterm vessel berths on Stewart St. and Roberts Bank in Vancouver, B.C.

The Orient Overseas Container Line claims its business in Vancouver and New York-New Jersey was particularly profitable in 2000. Its Long Beach terminal was twice cited as the "Best Container Terminal Operator in North America." Given Orient Overseas intimate ties to Beijing, U.S. intelligence agencies ought to have security interests in OOCL.

Chapter 7
A Clear and Present Danger

Every American port competes for ships and sells itself as "having quick turn-around times and efficient operating systems." Indeed, "the contest to have the most efficient and modern facilities is not new... Shipping lines are undergoing a lot of consolidation — and the competition... [can]...get even more intense... .[a] bidding war between East Coast ports erupted [in 1998] ...when Maersk Sealand, ..owned by the Danish industrial group A.P. Moller, threatened to move its hub out of New York," said Ken Cottrill, logistics and maritime editor at *Traffic World*.

"Everyone was falling all over themselves to offer them tax breaks and the best possible facilities," reported the *Atlanta Business Chronicle* of August 7, 2000.

Competition for business among America's ports is a national phenomena that has pushed considerations of national security entirely outside the scope of local thinking. USIC favors free markets and competition, but warns that local efforts to aid the China Ocean Shipping Company as a critical element of successful trade with China, may be costly to our country's defense.

"Los Angeles and Long Beach rule container traffic on the West Coast; in the East it's Norfolk, Virginia, and Charleston, South Carolina. For ships using the Gulf of Mexico …Houston is in high-stakes competition with New Orleans." [*Houston Press* July 7, 1998]

The Beijing-owned COSCO security problem is not confined to Long Beach/Los

Angeles, which first gave rise to public concerns. It is nationwide. COSCO ships sail in and out of American ports every day — Baltimore, Charleston, Houston, New York, Miami, New Orleans, Norfolk, Oakland, Port Elizabeth (NJ), Portland (OR), Seattle, Tacoma, and contiguous Vancouver, B.C.

A quiet private company with the extensive Beijing ties is the Orient Overseas Container Line. OOCL in the U.S. is headquartered in Pleasanton, California, around the San Francisco-Oakland Bay area. OOCL has service offices in the coastal cities of Boston, Charleston, Houston, Long Beach, New York, and Seattle and in Vancouver, B.C. and Panama. In addition to services in cities with OOCL offices, OOCL ships also deliver cargoes to Savannah, Norfolk, Miami, Los Angeles, and Oakland.

U.S. Customs is ill equipped to check any more than 2 percent of every cargo container — and then only if the paperwork is irregular or it has specific intelligence information. In fact, documents obtained by USIC show some

Chinese shipping firms have falsified their import papers.

As the Interagency Commission revealed, most American seaports have "fair to poor" security, rampant crime, corruption, and high vulnerability to terrorist attacks. It is in this context that it is prudent to alert the public and port authorities to the potential security risks presented by Beijing-owned COSCO and Beijing-intimate OOCL.

The U.S. Intelligence Council urges that more national security resources be devoted to preventing the export of U.S. military secrets to China. Moreover, USIC recommends that Congress and the Bush administration budget additional funds to the CIA, NSC, NSA, Customs, FBI and other agencies to halt such exports dangerous to our nation's survival.

USIC also urges the Bush administration and Congress to provide Customs with the resources necessary to perform its export control duties. For example, Custom's Automated Export System can account for only 39 percent of all U.S. exports and its Automated

Commercial System is near meltdown. A new Automated Commercial Environment system needs funding for $130 million.

At the very least, COSCO's ships and sailors must be considered as likely instruments of espionage as well as a source of revenue that will be used to modernize Red China's massive military machine. In the worst-case scenario, COSCO is the forward-deployed forces of a potential enemy who has already achieved a "stealth invasion" on our shores.

Right now, Red Chinese "front" companies like COSCO brazenly conduct their clandestine operations in our seaports because they're free from the scrutiny of U.S. authorities. These provide Beijing's agents with the perfect cover for:

- Intelligence gathering devices to spy on our navy
- Transportation to Red China of high-tech equipment stolen from America
- Concealed shipments into our country of arms, slave labor, prostitutes, drugs — or worse, weapons of mass destruction.

The China Ocean Shipping Company has already been caught red-handed running 2,000 illegal AK-47 assault rifles to LA street gangs — the largest seizure of automatic weapons in U.S. history. Beijing could easily blackmail America by smuggling nuclear, chemical or biological weapons right into a major seaport like Los Angeles.

The presence of nearly 100 ships of Red China's merchant marine and millions of unopened, uninspected containers entering the United States is a clear and present danger to American lives and property on our home shores.

Fortunately for the United States, we now have a president who recognizes that for too long Washington has turned a blind eye to this security gap. In a speech delivered to U.S. Navy personnel in Norfolk, Virginia, just weeks after his inauguration, George W. Bush stated, "With shared intelligence and enforcement, we must confront the threats that come in a shipping container or a suitcase."

Let us pray our leaders heed those words and that we're not too late in closing our gates to Red China's "Trojan Horse."

Postscript: After 9-11

A lot has changed since September 11, 2001. America's innocence was once again crushed by a dangerous world — evil in the form of terrorism supported by rogue states, many armed in part by Communist China.

Many of the controversial themes of *Stealth Invasion* are now accepted as established facts or at least prudent precautions.

- America is vulnerable to surprise attack in many places.

- Our enemies hate our civilization, our values, and our way of life.

- They will do unspeakable things.

- America must beef up homeland security.

- The President and many state and local officials must institute security measures at seaports, power plants, pipelines, and in cyberspace.

- America must carry its war against such evil far across the globe into the dens of terror.

- America must isolate terrorists from their state sponsors.

The initial signs are good. The sleeping giant has been awakened.

Airport security is being reformed. The U.S. Coast Guard is boarding commercial vessels. The U.S. Navy has moved vessels out of harm's way in U.S. ports. Critical infrastructures are being closed or guarded. Security has become a larger part of immigration policy. Security agencies are sharing intelligence.

Yet despite the Chinese knock down of an American plane in the South China Sea and the holding of American hostages in April 2001, there is insufficient recognition of the Red China threat so well documented by Bill Gertz, Steve Mosher, and others.

That being said, I am more optimistic about these matters than I have ever been.

I am hopeful that you will read *Stealth Invasion* and pass it on to others.

About the Author

Dr. Roger Canfield is executive director of the U.S. Intelligence Council. A respected political analyst and public information officer, he served as a public policy consultant for the California legislature from 1980-2000. Roger is a former daily political columnist for the *Sacramento Union* and former host of a radio talk show, "Under the Dome." His articles have been published in *Military, Human Events, National Review, New American, Dispatches, WorldNet Daily* and many newspapers. He received the "Medal of Patriotic Commander" from the families and survivors of the Nicaragua Resistance honoring his assistance in the liberation of the Nicaraguan people from Communist rule. He earned a Ph.D. in Government from the Claremont Graduate School and published his dissertation as *Black Ghetto Riots and Campus Disorders*. He has studied and taught international relations and, like his father, is a U.S. Navy veter-

an. Roger lives with his wife Noel in Fair
Oaks, California. They raised three children
and are now the proud grandparents of two
grandchildren. His book, *China Doll: Clinton,
Gore and the Selling of the U.S. Presidency*, co-
authored with USIC Chairman Richard A.
Delgaudio, has more than 700,000 copies in
print.

About USIC's Chairman

Richard A. Delgaudio, who serves as the U.S.
Intelligence Council's chairman of the board,
is president of the National Security Center
and the Legal Affairs Council. A leader in
conservative causes for more than 30 years, he
has made many TV and radio talk show
appearances. He is the author of the book,
Peril in Panama, and the forthcoming *China
Beachhead.* A participant and sponsor of
numerous fact-finding missions to Panama,
he presented testimony to Congress on the
issue of Communist Chinese interests in the
Panama Canal. He is a former Senior National
Director of Young Americans for Freedom

and, later, YAF Alumni Chairman and National Advisory Board Member. A devoted father, he enjoys skiing, scuba diving and Tae Kwon Do with his three children.

How to Contact Them

Dr. Canfield and Mr. Delgaudio are available as speakers on the subject of this book. While they do not require an honorarium, travel expenses would be appreciated. Both are also available for radio talk show interviews and appreciate the help of fellow patriots in securing such engagements. You can contact them at:

U.S. Intelligence Council
Office of the Chairman
10560 Main St., Suite 217
Fairfax, VA, 22030
(801-640-3466)

The U.S. Intelligence Council's Mission

Founded to safeguard the national security of America from enemies both foreign and domestic, the United States Intelligence Council performs its mission through the collection and dissemination of information to interested American citizens.

The Council researches and gathers material important to the security, defense, economic and sovereign interests of the nation.

USIC takes an active role in encouraging citizens to communicate regularly with their national elected leaders and appointed office-holders on those issues.

You Can Help USIC Lobby Congress

The Council encourages citizens to regularly communicate with their U.S. Senators and their Congressman on these issues. For inquiry to your U.S. Senator or U.S.

Congressman, you may telephone the Capitol Switchboard, (202) 224-3121.

For those interested in accessing additional information about our elected officials via the Internet, please see the U.S. Senate Internet Home Page http://www.senate.gov, and U.S. House of Representatives Internet Home page http://www.house.gov.

Please write to your two U.S. Senators and to your Representative concerning the matters raised in this publication:

Honorable (name of Senator)
United States Senate
Washington, DC 20510-2203
Salutation "Dear Senator (name):"

Honorable (name of Representative)
United States House of Representatives
Washington, DC 20515-1101
Salutation "Dear Congressman (name):"

We also strongly encourage you to support the work of the U.S. Intelligence Council, including continued distribution of this publication and others like it, by sending your donation (not tax deductible) to:

United States Intelligence Council
P.O. Box 919
Frederick, MD 21705-09190

How You Can Help Defend America from Future Terrorist Attacks

This book can have a powerful impact on our country's national security and America's future — if you and others act now. Please give copies to your family and friends so all patriotic citizens can learn the truth about Red China's "stealth invasion."

By distributing as many copies as you can, you will be supporting one of the U.S. Intelligence Council's most important grassroots educational campaigns, and you could be helping decide the fate of American history. This has never been more important than now, in the wake of the September 11, 2001 terrorist assault on the United States and her innocent citizens.

Stealth Invasion Order Form

❏ Single Copy $4.95 ❏ Two Copies $8.00
❏ Three Copies $11.00

(Please add a $2 shipping and handling fee
to your total. A special bulk 40% discount
rate is available to booksellers and orders of
100 books, plus $20 shipping and handling.)

Please send me_____copies of the book,
*Stealth Invasion: Red Chinese Operations in
North America*. Enclosed is my check for
$_____ payable to USIC.

Name:_____

Address:_____

City:_____

State:_____ ZIP:_____

**U.S. Intelligence Council
Office of the Chairman
10560 Main St., Suite 217
Fairfax, VA, 22030**

The United States Intelligence Council is incorporated under the
IRS code as a 501(c) 4 non-profit corporation and relies solely on the
contributions of individuals to support its research and lobbying
efforts. Your non-tax deductible donation may be made payable to
USIC and is greatly appreciated.

Stealth Invasion Order Form

❏ Single Copy $4.95   ❏ Two Copies $8.00
❏ Three Copies $11.00

(Please add a $2 shipping and handling fee
to your total. A special bulk 40% discount
rate is available to booksellers and orders of
100 books, plus $20 shipping and handling.)

Please send me _____ copies of the book,
*Stealth Invasion: Red Chinese Operations in
North America*. Enclosed is my check for
$ _____ payable to USIC.

Name: _____

Address: _____

City: _____

State: _____ ZIP: _____

U.S. Intelligence Council
Office of the Chairman
10560 Main St., Suite 217
Fairfax, VA, 22030

Other U.S. Intelligence Council Publications

Books:
China Doll: Clinton, Gore and the Selling of the U.S. Presidency

Reports:
China Traders: Assessing the Legacy of Clinton-Gore's Appeasement Policy, U.S. National Security at Risk

What Red China Got for Its Money (Why did the People's Republic of China Invest in the 1996 Reelection Campaign of President Bill Clinton?)